THE JOY OF SOCKS

MAGGIE DRUMMOND

With illustrations by Gerald Rose

Foreword by Sophie Mirman

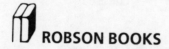 ROBSON BOOKS

First published in Great Britain in 1988 by Robson Books Ltd,
Bolsover House, 5—6 Clipstone Street, London W1P 7EB

Text copyright © 1988 Maggie Drummond
Illustrations copyright © 1988 Gerald Rose
Jacket and text design by Linda Wade

British Library Cataloguing in Publication Data
Drummond, Maggie
 The joy of socks.
 1. Hosiery——Anecdotes, satire, etc.
 I. Title
 646.4'2 GT2128

ISBN 0 86051 552 4

Printed in Great Britain by St Edmundsbury Press Ltd, Bury St Edmunds,
Suffolk

Typeset by Bookworm Typesetting, Manchester

FOREWORD

Are marriages made in heaven? I believe that the responsibility lies somewhere north-west of Leicester within a small enclave where factories are busy churning out socks. Ah, you may ask, what does this have to do with marriage? It is only through misinterpretation and poor reporting over the years by hard-of-hearing journalists that the major reason for the failure of marriages has been cited as an 'irretrievable breakdown of sex or non consummation'. The major reason should of course be 'irretrievable breakdown in socks or utter consternation'.

How absurd to talk about a marriage on the rocks! What have rocks got to do with relationships? Marriage on the socks is what it's all about, meaning a loving, caring relationship full of joyful darning and footsie under the table.

I am very proud to have been asked to write the Foreword to this book as it is the first of its type not to have been sold in a plain, brown, sealed envelope. If only Dr Spock had been more forthcoming and written under his real name of Dr Sock. Can you imagine the effect that *Baby and Foot Care* would have had on the last two generations?

I am equally proud to earn my living in the business of socraphilia, a previously dubious pastime which, thanks to the author of this book, is now socially acceptable. What started out as an underground operation has now come out into the open and Sock Shops are to be found in most liberated and forward-thinking places in the United Kingdom.

To those of you new to the Joy of Socks I welcome you to a wonderful world. It is a truly pleasurable experience which will stay long in the memory. To those of you already committed I take this opportunity to thank you for your support and hope you will continue to spread the word. To the author of this most serious thesis, many congratulations on what has obviously been years of hard labour and the result is no mean feet.

Sophie Mirman

Chairman and Joint Managing
Director of Sock Shop

INTRODUCTION

Some years ago I wrote an article in *The Times* complaining how impossible it was to both work and stay at home with the children. I had reached crisis point. The following week, I opened the newspaper to find my husband complaining about the problems of life with a working wife.

It was the little things in life that mattered – the little things that went astray. Where, he wanted to know, were his SOCKS?

'When you are trying to persuade the chairman of a £100m company to unravel his accounts and his eyes glaze over as he spots one white tennis sock peeping from beneath your pin-stripe, then you appreciate the real significance of socks in pairs,' he wrote. But did I?

Those socks haunted us – and the letter columns of *The Times* – for weeks. There was clearly more to socks than met the feet.

As one woman reader wrote: 'Mismatched socks are a terrible indication of low status. A man with a keen sense of position is not seen publicly in one white sock and one black one. We all recognize that status is important to the male psyche.' Socks was a feminist issue, said another. Can we afford to waste our time on them? 'After all in an age of high technology and keen competition, who will consider employing anyone with 20 years of sock-sorting experience?' Men readers sympathized with my husband, offering practical solutions – and in one case, a new pair of socks.

Katherine Whitehorn summed it up in the *Observer*. Was the debate about sockage – the trouble with socks,

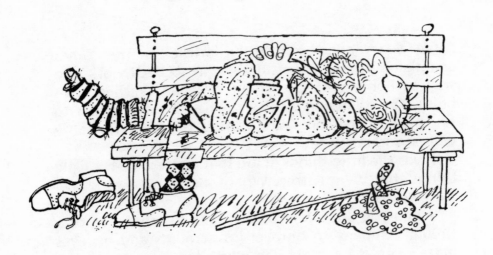

or soccage – a feudal word meaning an obligation to pay homage at the court of a superior?

This book is for every woman who has ever wondered the same thing – and for every man who has failed to find a clean matching pair of socks in the morning. Particularly my husband, Michael Walters.

I would like to thank the following socks enthusiasts for their help: Christopher Fildes, Sebastian Doggart, Oliver Sellers, Robin and Micheline Ellison, Michael Walters, Tim and Peter Hall, Sally White and Liz Walker, George Gale and Elizabeth Rose.

THE HISTORY OF SOCKS

IN THE BEGINNING
... there was socks – just about

From the very dawn of history, socks were on the wrong foot. The word 'sock' in classical Greek plays originally referred to the light shoe worn by comic actors. The 'sock' of comedy was short – only to the ankle, while the 'buskin' of tragedy came up to the knee. As a result 'sock' came to be used as a word for comedy itself:

> *Then to the well-trod stage anon,*
> *If Jonson's learned sock be on*
> Milton, *L'Allegro*

This doesn't mean that Jonson was actually wearing socks on stage – the sock is the play itself.

AD 1-1589 THE LOST YEARS

For hundreds and hundreds of years, people were very ignorant about socks. The upper classes wore tights or stockings. As a result, socks were very much looked down upon. You only wore them if you could not afford to go all the way with a proper pair of stockings. The mass of the peasantry had to make do with various unsavoury footbindings – or go barefoot, with no socks at all. You had to work very hard to join the AriSOCKracy, since all socks had to be made by hand.

---

footnote The earliest example of recorded socks is a surviving pair from 6th or 7th century Egypt.

1589–1820 THE SOCKS REVOLUTION

The socks revolution started in 1589 when a Notting-hamshire curate, the Reverend William Lee, invented the first knitting machine, enabling people to get more socks, faster. The English, however, did not cotton on to socks immediately – the Reverend Lee was forced by apathy to take his invention to France where ideas about socks seemed to be much more advanced even then.

But socks themselves remained fairly crude – they had to be cut and stitched up at the sides.

1820 The invention of a machine for circular knitting was the start of a new era of Socks For All. Despite the Luddites' fierce opposition to the arrival of the modern industrial sockciety, their resistance was crushed under-foot. By the end of the 19th century, mass-produced socks were cheap, factory-made and easily obtainable.

1900–1988

This was the great socks era. Socks really came out of hiding. Men went socks-mad in the 1920s and '30s. The popularity of plus-fours (trousers which gave up just below the knee) meant they could now shake a leg in all kinds of patterned and coloured footwear.

But two World Wars changed people's socks lives for ever. Rationing meant that everyone went short of socks for a while. Ankle-high austerity socks became the order of the day, leaving a gaping hole in people's lives.

1940s and '50s Socks triumphed over the law of gravity. The invention of man-made fibres meant they could stay up longer without visible means of support.

1960s The Permissive Sockciety introduced alternative socks – psychedelic socks – spotted socks – multicoloured socks. People even gave up socks as a protest against the prevailing materialistic culture.

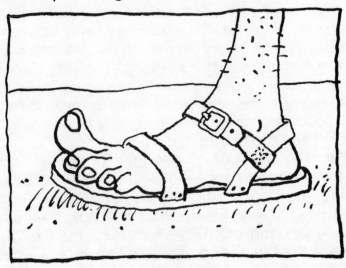

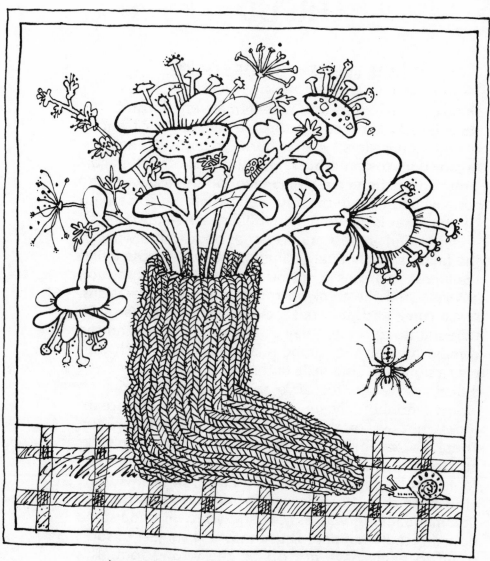

◦ Still Life with Sock ◦

FREUD

ARE WE AFREUD OF SOCKS?

The crucial role of socks in male/female relationships has been largely ignored by the massed ranks of agony aunts, counsellors, behavioural scientists, doctors, Archbishops of Canterbury, feminists and other luminaries who have been crashingly silent on this aspect of the human condition, in the mistaken belief that something known as sex is the dominant influence in relationships.

This underlying assumption goes back to the work of the famous psychoanalyst Sigmund Freud, whose belief that most neuroses could be explained in this fashion has coloured the thinking of subsequent generations. Freud completely ignored socks. How relevant can such thinking be to present-day attempts to understand the complexities of one-to-one relationships in which they play a significant but little understood role?

Indeed, if Freud were alive and waffling on today he would undoubtedly be discussing the importance of socks – not sex – as the mainspring of human behaviour. There is a possibility he may have been discussing socks all along, but has been poorly served by interpreters fooled by his foreign accent. Try saying 'socks' with the kind of thick guttural intonation favoured by German Commandants in war movies and you will understand how this could happen. Thus the whole subject of socks could so easily have got off on the wrong foot. This theory certainly explains some baffling aspects of socks behaviour – the tendency to stray, the lack of pair bonding, the seemingly intrinsic incompatibility. Not to mention the extraordinarily obsessive behaviour commonly observed in the average male when he cannot find any socks in the morning.

It might explain, too, the high divorce rate – of both socks and people. Alas, we may never know the real truth about Freud and socks.

MARITAL SOCKS

'Arthur said, "I like being married. I want everyone I care about to be married."

"You just want everyone to be in the same pot you're in," said Mark.

"I like the pot I'm in," said Arthur. "I like how it goes along. What's for dinner and which movie should we see and where are my socks."

"Where are your socks?" said Mark. "Where are my socks? Where are all the missing socks?"

"They're in heaven," said Arthur. "You die, you go to heaven and they bring you a big box and it's got all your lost socks in it and you get to spend eternity sorting them all out." '

from *Heartburn* by Norah Ephron

' "Socks," said Emma-Audrey to Jocelyn. "Socks. Two male children and one man. Six socks a day seven days a week. Forty-two socks a week. Why? Why do they wear them, and worse, who do I feel obliged to wash them?" '

from *Down Among the Women* by Fay Weldon

SOCKS TALK

All a man really means to say about socks, but is too embarrassed to say out loud.

Have you noticed HOW MUCH TIME men spend talking and thinking about, let alone wearing, socks? How socks is frequently the focal point of male dissatisfaction with the vicissitudes of life? Arguments about socks may not be as trivial as they seem. When a man says, 'For heaven's sake, I can't even find a decent pair of socks in this house', he may not be having a rational conversation about the lack of feetwear *per se*, or even exhibiting the well-known male inability to see what is right in front of him.

Subconsciously, he could be making a serious value-laden statement (usually an impolite one) about the impact of post-feminist philosophy on male/female relationships in the later decades of the twentieth century. Here's how to unravel the deeper meaning of socks.

'I haven't got a pair' means 'We are not a pair'.

'I just don't understand why there are never any socks' means 'I know you care more about your career than my comfort'.

'I don't ask for much – only a pair of socks' means 'I'll marry a slave girl next time around'.

'I wonder where this odd sock came from' means 'You've gone and lost the other one, haven't you?'

'Isn't this the pair I was wearing yesterday?' means 'You are the pits'.

'Or, I'm seeing my solicitor about a divorce'.

· Sir Cyril ·

· Maggie Thatcher ·

· Lord Lucan ·

· Jeffrey Archer ·

· Nell Gwynn ·

· Prince Charles ·

18

ODD SOCKS

Some words of comfort for every man who has ever looked down and wondered *'Am I odd? Am I different this morning?'*

Few things (adultery, non-ironed shirts, chicken breasts for dinner *again*) inspire such feelings of guilt and frustration or provoke such mutual suspicion and recrimination in an otherwise perfectly matched couple as a pile of odd socks.

Women see odd socks as a challenge to their domestic competence. Men moan about them as part of life's natural disorder.

What happens to the other, lost sock of the pair is one of the great mysteries of our time. Yet despite the fact that most of us live within easy walking distance of at least 30 odd socks, no one has yet made a proper scientific study of why you can put a dozen pairs in the wash and get 10 and a half pairs back plus one sock you have never seen before.

It is difficult to under-estimate the scale of the problem. If the 24 million sock-wearing males in the UK lose just one sock during the course of a year (and on the basis of anecdotal evidence this is a modest assumption), the implication is that there are at least 24 million socks on the loose at any one time. Indeed, there are probably more socks wandering around on their own than in pairs. You are not alone in your odd socks.

Socks loss is quite different from other home hazards. The loss of a shirt or a pair of underpants may pass un-noticed. A shirt is solo, and can thus disappear by itself without trace. Underpants may be a pair, but always travel in tandem. No *under* can be left *pant*ing for a partner. The odd sock, on the other hand, hangs around as a singular rebuke, a constant reminder of what might have been, engendering a sense of loss and failure.

This is compounded by the practice in many house-holds of allowing the odd socks to linger on, in the hopes that the partners will return, instead of just throwing them away and forgetting about them. This is a common neurosis known to socks theorists as ma-SOCKism. This syndrome is particularly common amongst women. There is only one cure for this condition. Put all the odd socks in a bag and *throw them away*. NOW.

Odd socks are not, of course, intrinSOCKally odd – most are extremely conservative, even boring in appearance, and their appearance is so frequent that it is hard to see why we should ever regard them as odd – why not mismatched, or singles, independent, or some other less hurtful expression used to describe anyone or anything that has problems with maintaining a pair-bonding relationship?

They are called odd merely because they usually pop up in peculiar, SOCKluded places, often looking slightly shrunk and wrinkled. Favourite sock hiding places are: behind the bread bin, in the corner of the duvet cover, in the children's toy cupboard, on the stairs, under the bed, in the washing-machine pump, and occasionally down the backs of sofas, from which they are destined to be retrieved by unthinking houseguests on their third gin and tonic. Socks found in the back seat of a car should be viewed with extreme suspicion.

The crucial question is: are odd socks the result of

human error? Or does the real problem lie with the nature of socks (or for the purpose of this discussion) *the sock* itself?

While the first proposition seems to offer a rational solution, the empirical evidence is by no means conclusive. It does not, for instance, explain why, if you buy lots of socks in the same style and colour, subtle differences appear after a time. It does not account for *where* you find odd socks – how they get where they are, and why they get lost singly rather than in pairs. In fact, the more socks you own, the odder they become, simply because there are more to go missing. This unfortunate mathematical progression is known as The Law of Haverages.

MYTHING SOCKS

Since so little is really known about the Odd Sock Syndrome, myths flourish. Hence the oft-heard early-morning cry of the deprived male: *'Why are my socks mything?'*

Men have socks on the brain. Hence the topic seems to inspire all manner of irrational and childish beliefs.

MYTH NO. 1

Washing machines eat socks, thanks to a peculiar process known as SOCKtion.

Not a scrap of scientific evidence exists to support this, but the myth would appear to be particularly prevalent among bachelors who take their socks to the launderette, watch them spinning round, and always discover one or more missing when they get home. The logical explanation is that they simply fail to check the machine properly after use, leaving odd socks behind them.

MYTH NO. 2

The Random Walk *theory of socks presupposes that socks have a life of their own, wandering hither and thither at will, and that there is very little we can do about it.*

Random walk theorists are frequently followers of Eastern religions, many of whom wear no socks at all. Others may demonstrate a passive attitude to the wearing of odd socks, which is frequently all they can get. No one, of course, has actually *witnessed* a sock on the move. The more logical explanation is that whoever started this myth used the launderette straight after the chap who invented Myth No. 1.

MYTH NO. 3

Women withhold socks deliberately. This theory is too silly for words.

Do **YOU** have Socks Appeal?

Stylish and SOCKcessful – or always the odd one out? Are you one of a matching pair – or is there always something missing? Does your loved one see you as a socks symbol? – How is your socks life? Should you do something to freshen it up? Test your SOCKS APPEAL and find your true pairsonality with the help of our intimate questionnaire.

When you make love do you take your socks off
- a Before
- b During
- c Only when the light's off?

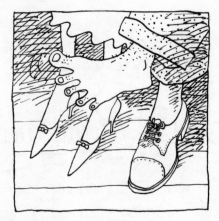

Do you believe in playing FOOTSIE?
- a On a first date
- b Only after SHE slips HER shoes off
- c When it means the Financial Times Stock Exchange Index
  – but only in a bare market.

What do you think is the key ingredient for socks satisfaction?
- a Variety – trying lots of different kinds of socks
- b Compatibility – sticking to the same socks in a long-standing relationship
- c Availability – you feel pathetically grateful whenever opportunity socks.

When socks let you down, do you blame
[a] the feminist movement
[b] the washing machine
[c] your big feet

When you tell your partner you need socks urgently, do they
[a] offer some without hesitation
[b] say they've got a headache
[c] accuse you of being a socks maniac

How you SCORE at SOCKS

$a = 5$ $b = 2$ $c = 0$

25–15

You never have ANY trouble with socks do you? Any time, anywhere, women seem to throw them at your feet – other men envy your amazing socks technique. Striped, spotted or fluorescent, you aren't afraid to experiment with socks. Your only problem is that you get quickly bored walking around as part of a pair.

15–5

You really like to come home after a hard day's work and find your socks all ready and waiting for you – you never really enjoyed being footloose and fancy-free – you really view socks in terms of a caring, sharing couple. Occasionally you may be tempted – who isn't – by other superficially attractive socks on offer, but basically what you want out of life is a clean matching pair in the morning.

0

You really take your feet in hand and get your socks life sorted out. Only then can you expect to find someone who is prepared to do it for you. Currently your self esteem seems to have slipped down around your ankles.

SOCKS THERAPY

Walking around with wet feet is such a miserable experience it is hard to believe anyone would do it deliberately. Hydrotherapy experts disagree. They believe wet sock treatments can be a powerful force in relieving stress — and help cure insomnia. The wet sock technique was developed by a nineteenth-century Bavarian priest called Kneipp, famous for his water treatments, which are widely used even today to cure aches and pains. It is all designed to relax you at the end of a long hard day. Itching to try?

First, soak a pair of cotton socks in cold water, then wring them out. Slide them on to your feet. Put a pair of *dry* wool socks on over them, and then go to bed for at least half an hour. If you wish, or perhaps if you don't, you can keep them on all night since the object of the exercise is to send you to sleep.

SOCKSERCISE

Forget aerobics and jogging – you can get all the exercise you need just putting your socks on each morning with the help of SOCKSercise – THE new fitness programme guaranteed to turn the average slob into a masculine hunk in a few simple steps. No diets, no pills, no special equipment – just a pair of socks, two feet, and a positive mental attitude. Here's how to get phy-SOCKal:

Warm Up   a few gentle movements are always recommended before any strenuous activity so that the muscles can adapt themselves gradually:

a) Put socks on bedroom radiator.

b) Touch toes five times.

c) Raise knee to chin five times.

You are then ready to start your SOCKSercises – check you are in the correct posture with our easy-to-follow RIGHT/WRONG diagrams.

1. THE LEGOVER POSITION

This is an easy SOCKSercise for the complete beginner. Sit on the edge of the bed, and lift right foot on to the left knee sideways. Put the sock on the right foot and pull up towards the calf, putting the strain on your stomach muscles. Repeat with left leg on right knee. The advanced form of this SOCKSercise is achieved by trying to put your big toe in your mouth.

2. THE ONE FOOT WONDER

Once you have mastered the simple legover technique, you can move to the intermediate stage, which is performed standing up: Stand with bottom against a wall or door, holding sock in both hands. Raise left leg, bending at the knee, and rest heel against right knee. Bend at waist and put left toe in sock – any excess air in body will be expelled during this manoeuvre. Pull up sock while returning left leg to floor – slowly and agonizingly to the count of six. Repeat, raising right leg.

Then try doing it without balancing heel on the opposite knee. Ha ha. Thought that would happen.

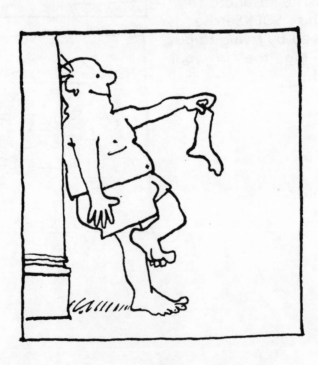

3. THE FLOOR ROLL

Remain on floor, and roll over on back with sock in left hand and legs flat. Lift right leg up, keeping it straight, and simultaneously raise both arms in direction of feet, thus raising shoulders. Bend right knee and roll forward, bringing shoulders off the ground, tugging sock on quickly. Return to starting position. Then repeat, raising left leg. For the advanced form of this SOCKSercise, try lifting both legs at the same time. Feel ridiculous? This SOCKSercise is guaranteed to stretch your sense of humour. If nothing else.

MEDICAL WARNING. SOCKSercise should not be attempted by anyone who experiences physical discomfort getting their socks on in the normal fashion. Test your suitability for the programme with the following: sit cross-legged on floor, and place one leg behind your neck. If you find you cannot get your socks on from this position, you should see your doctor immediately.

SMELLY SOCKS – THE WHIFF OF CONTROVERSY

One perennial problem that exercises the minds of serious socks experts, or indeed anyone who cannot afford or conjure up a clean pair for every day of the week, is SMELLY SOCKS – universally acknowledged to have a tang similar to very ripe cheese. This fragrance, highly prized in a Gorgonzola, is considered extremely bad form at foot level. Posh socksmakers claim that man-made fibre socks are particularly prone to smelliness.

Unlike more expensive varieties manufactured in cotton, silk, or wool, the artificial fibre does not allow the foot to breathe. The man-made socksmen claim there are no such things as smelly socks, only smelly feet – but they would, wouldn't they?

Attempts have been made to manufacture pong-free socks that could be worn several times on the trot by treating them with special chemicals that make them resistant to bacteria. The Consumers Association actually carried out a series of feet trials to test if these worked. *Which* magazine duly reported the findings:

'We asked 11 volunteers to wear matched socks, one treated, one untreated. They didn't know which of the socks was which. We organized a panel of three blindfold sniffers (also volunteers. Incidentally we found that willing footsniffers were few and far between). The sock wearers presented first their feet,

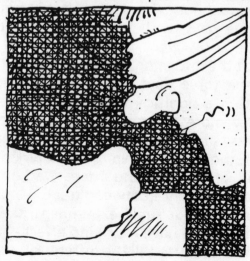

then their socks, for sniffing. In each case one foot or sock was presented twice, the other once, in random order. Each footsniffer was asked to detect which was the odd one out. The socks were worn for three consecutive days, with sniffing tests at the end of each. The socks were not washed. The feet were washed at the discretion of each volunteer.

Over the three days the sniffers picked the 'odd man out' in a significant number of times. In these cases they more often picked out treated socks as being less smelly than they did untreated ones. However, the sniffers often failed to pick out the 'odd man out' at all, showing there was not an easily detectable difference between treated and untreated socks. So from our small experiment, the treatment does not seem to have a striking effect – you have to sniff very carefully to tell the difference.'

SOCK'S LAW

1. Socks are bought in twos – but disappear in ones.

2. Men wear socks – but only wives lose them.

3. Husbands can see differences in a pair of apparently perfectly-matched socks that are undetectable to the normal human eye.

4. Buy a dozen pairs of identical socks and two months later you will have 23 odd ones instead. This does not happen the other way round.

5. By the time you have found a lost sock, you will have forgotten where the hell you put the odd one.

6. No two odd socks are ever the same.

7. There is always a long red woolly one lurking in the corner.

The Sock of the New *– with apologies to Harpers and Queen*

High? Higher? **Too high?** *The fashion world is divided as designers pull up our socks to new dizzy heights ... It's the* **sock of the new** *this season as feet get on the* **move** *again ... turning in a different* **direction** *– where angels fear to tread ... so bold ... so brave ... so* **inconSOCKuential** *... this season's* **big message** *is up up and away for today's fashion victim putting his* **best dressed foot forward.**

London ... Rome ... Paris ... Milan ... Anklesey ... everywhere expresses the new **mood** *... the new* **feeling** *about* **socks** *...* **hot passionate colours** *... of noisy socks ...* **or the pale but interesting leg** *... with* **new** *fichu kneeline or* **paired down** *strictness ... that tells us what we think about socks ...* **now.**

So ... Renew you sock options this season *– you'll love the new* **legginess,** *you'll adore the new* **tendon**ness *of lengthening stretches of navy bri-nylon clinging lasciviously from knee to ankle ... so much more socks ... so much more macho ... so* **mucha more money** *to spend on ridiculous clothes.*

*But of course **more** . . . socks means **less** . . .*
trousers . . . now Paris demands that legs are
chopped off just below the knee to emphasize
*the new **calf love** . . . as men express their new*
*freedom . . . ushering in the new **permissive***
***SOCKciety** . . . uttering the new*
*fashion statement . . . we love the **new** socks.*

*Socks are **in** – trousers are very nearly **off***
– either abandoned altogether . . . till
reappearing much much higher up the leg . . .
sometimes swathed . . . sometimes ruched . . .
*hardly trousers at all really **but** – fiercely*
tailored for day . . . softly draped by night
. . . think of Sir Francis Drake – or Lord
Baden-Powell . . . or any half-witted
pretentious reference that comes into
your head.

***But** how far should you go with socks?*
*Just **so** far . . . or we say **all the way***
*. . . It's up to **you, your conscience, and***
your legs.

SOCKS EDUCATION A PARENTS' GUIDE
by Dr Sock

THE BABY STAGE

The pressures of modern life mean that boys are aware of socks from an increasingly early age. The male socks life starts in the cradle – when he is given his ritual initiation by the elders – he is forced into a pair of blue bootees knitted by grandmother, one size too small. It is quite normal for baby to go through a phase of rejection as he attempts to kick off his first pair of socks. Baby socks are small and easily lost. Parents may find it useful to tie the bootees together. This may sound rather cruel, but it is a crucial stage of socks development; an early lesson in the art of keeping socks in pairs.

PRE-SCHOOL

Young boys show a great desire to experiment with socks. Often this takes the form of wearing socks as mittens instead of on their feet, or attempting to put a sock over the head of the family cat. At this stage in his development, a young child has little interest in the meaning of socks, and sees no point in wearing them. They simply get in the way of favourite activities, like chewing his big toenail. Introduce your child to socks one by one.

THE OVER-FIVES

At this stage, parents can leave the question of socks safely to school. There he will be introduced to socks as an essential element of adult life. The average school uniform list, for instance, is guaranteed to empty the sock counter of your local chain store.

The standard school socks curriculum should include:
>   Short grey socks (6 pairs)
>   Short grey best socks (2 pairs) for Sundays and school trips
>   Rugby socks in school colours, 1 pair autumn term
>   Cricket socks (white) 1 pair summer term (an extra pair in special school colours required if son is in school team)
>   Gym socks (short white)

A child's school sock maintenance requirements, however, are comparatively modest. One welcome feature of school socks is that they are rarely brought home for a wash, except at the end of term (when there will be relatively few of them left). Children are not possessive about socks, and appear to be very happy wearing everyone else's. The traditional practice of sewing on name tapes has now been discredited as a complete waste of time, though it is useful in the first few weeks for those with an identity crisis.

PUBERTY and ADOLESCENCE

The onset of puberty means dramatic changes in your child's attitude to socks. He will become shy and secretive – hiding socks away in the corners of his wardrobe and beneath his bed. He may become increasingly socks conscious – wanting to choose his own socks rather than take what is offered. You must respect his independence – but always be there with a pair of socks for him when he needs you.

UNIVERSITY SOCKS

Be prepared for the onslaught of socks and drugs and rock'n'roll. Even when your son leaves home, he will frequently bring his socks back to visit you. A high degree of tolerance may be required if he pairs up with something too flashy and awful. Odd couples may soon drift apart. You may be tested by experiments with shared socks, communal socks, radical socks, even left-only socks. Consult your doctor if he should start smoking socks.

HOPSOCKS
An Adult Game

An Adult Game

This is a grown-up version of the well-known children's yard game, using socks not stones. It is just the thing to break the ice at a party – or to settle the digestion after a really good lunch. You need to mark out the standard 10 square hopsock circuit, and find any number of able-bodied socks wearers to participate. The winner is the first player to complete the circuit and end up with the correct pair of socks back on his or her feet. In view of the fact that the game involves hopping with bare feet, a soft surface (grass) is preferable to a hard one. Anyone who falls over in the course of the game is automatically OUT, and has to go home without their socks on. In addition there are penalty points – the loss of one sock for landing on the wrong square.

TO START   Each player takes off his or her socks. For the purposes of this game it is important that the socks are *matching,* and that each player wears a different, easily recognizable colour to prevent cheating. The referee then turns the socks into a ball shape and the game begins.

HOPSOCKS

ORDER OF PLAY   is decided by each player throwing the sock ball over the shoulder onto the circuit. The player who throws the sock ball on the highest square starts first, and the rest follow on the same principle.

THE GAME   The player can throw the sock ball on *any* of the numbered squares and hop to retrieve it. But you can only unravel the ball and retrieve your own sock if it falls on square numbers 2, 3, 5, 6 or 8, 9. As you can now see the challenge of the game is to retrieve your sock, and put it back on your foot while standing on one leg – in squares 1, 4, 7 or 10. You must unravel the ball, put your sock on, and reform the ball before you can hop over the rest of the circuit. *This is much harder than it sounds*. The winner is the first player to get both socks on – theoretically possible in two rounds.

RULES   You lose one or both socks if you pinch someone else's by mistake, have two feet on the ground during retrieval, or fall over. The referee's decision is final.

THE MID-LIFE CRISIS

Even the most easy-going, compatible pair of socks can suffer from A Mid-life Crisis after a few years' wear and tear. The signs are easy to spot:

A sock may get very out of shape, developing a paunchy, wrinkled appearance.

A sock may have difficulty staying up for as long as it used to.

A sock may grow apart from its mate.

A sock may not cling to you as it once did.

A sock may make a fool of itself trying to pair up with something younger and more exotic in silk or cashmere.

There is no easy cure. Old age comes to us all. With advancing years, our interest in socks wanes. One solution is to give your socks a complete break. Put them in a drawer away from it all, in the hope that they will recover. Another is a change of career to something less stressful. Even if they are no longer smart enough for daily wear, they can still play a valuable role around the garden in a pair of wellington boots.

THE GOOD SOCKS GUIDE

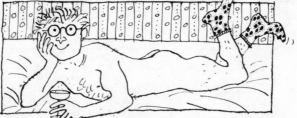

Are you part of the Feet Elite – or do your socks let you down? Men rarely see their feet as others see them. When you look in the mirror to check shirt, tie, or the cut of a jacket, socks are simply not in the frame. When you are sitting down in company, however, socks are *very* noticeable to the person sitting opposite. Here's a handy guide to what's IN and what should be OFF.

WHAT'S IN

SAFE SOCKS Finely knit black cotton, going up the calf, ending just below the knee. The footmark of the perfect gentleman. Black can be worn with virtually any kind of business suit.

NAVY SOCKS can be worn only if they are *very dark,* practically black. Most navy socks look like school uniform.

WHITE SOCKS can be worn with jeans and loafers, but only by the very young, beautiful, rich (you need lots of pairs) and obviously heterosexual.

RED SOCKS Socks for the Thinking Man. Red socks definitely cut a dash when worn with an absolutely impeccably cut, impeccably traditional pin-striped suit. Red socks should only be worn when you have your feet firmly on the career ladder and want to be *noticed*.

CANARY YELLOW can be worn by the Talented Eccentric when he's run out of red socks, but still wants to make a point with his feet.

WHAT'S OFF

SHORT SOCKS Few things are more unattractive than a sudden display of six inches of hairy white leg. If you MUST wear short socks, DON'T sit down.

BROWN SOCKS are always a foul colour, but thick hand-knitted, hairy ones are OK for shooting.

TWO-TONE SOCKS Like black with a single stripe of blue, these are horribly mediocre.

PATTERNED SOCKS Unless they are REALLY WITTY.

You should NEVER have socks with shorts or sandals, unless you are prepared to wear a white knotted handkerchief on your head.

SOCK WORDS & PHRASES

SOCK is not just something you put on your feet. It appears to have a wide variety of alternative meanings. As you might expect, few of them seem to go together.

SOCK is still used at Eton as a word for sweets. Like most Etonian traditions no one seems to know quite how this one started. The term came into use around the mid-19th century and stuck. One theory is that it goes back to a time when sweets were banned, and Etonians hid them in their socks. That may also explain why some Old Etonians have odd tastes. Another theory is that a gang of bullies once went round Rowland's, the school sweet shop, threatening people that unless they were given money they would be socked in the face. Either explanation could be right – or left.

SOCKS AND VIOLENCE

SOCK is well established as meaning a knock or a blow – as in the phrase 'to sock somebody one', which is still current today.

In the 1920s, the word SOCKO was used to describe a prize fight. Hence the expression 'I knocked the socks off him', meaning you have won a decisive victory.

The word SOCKDOLOGER, too, means a truly decisive blow in US Wild West vocabulary.

A SOCKER meant a lout, simpleton, or hooligan. These days, of course, it is often spelt 'soccer'.

SOCK also meant something more pleasant. Between 1805 and 1845 it was widely used to mean confectionery or something nice to eat. Then it acquired a more general meaning as a treat, eg, 'I'll sock you to a movie' – from *A Handful of Dust* by Evelyn Waugh.

SOCKS AND MONEY

Sock also has a financial meaning, but it is not clear whether this derives from the folk tradition of people keeping their savings in their socks. There are instances of sock meaning pocket. But SOCKET MONEY was a 17th-century word meaning money given and received on marriage. A SOCKETER was a 19th-century word for a blackmailer. In American slang, sock can mean to save money, as in 'sock it away'. A third explanation of sock at Eton is that it meant buying your goodies on credit.

WINDSOCKS have been used since the early days of aviation to help pilots to judge the strength and direction of the wind. When flying conditions were so bad because of fog that even the windsock on the mast was invisible the airfield was described as SOCKED IN. No planes could land or take off.

BOBBYSOCKS – 1950s short (bobbed) white socks worn by teenagers (bobbysoxers).

SOCKHOP – 1950s teenage party where adolescents danced without their shoes.

PUT A SOCK IN IT – means 'stop talking about it'. Originally a US army expression from the late 19th century, it is widely used here. Not an invitation to stuff a pair of socks in your mouth, it is more likely to mean a threat of violence. Or perhaps chew a sweet and shut up.

PULL YOUR SOCKS UP – try harder, don't slacken – British Army, 1910.

SOCK IT TO ME – 'hit me with it'. This phrase was made famous on both sides of the Atlantic in the late '60s by the TV comedy show, Rowan and Martin's *Laugh In*. Whoever said it had a bucket of water thrown over

his or her head, or suffered some similar indignity. It was used ad nauseam by disc jockeys. But it was apparently used, if not invented, by Mark Twain in the late 19th century, and subsequently became part of the vocabulary of negro jazz musicians.

BLESS YOUR LITTLE COTTON SOCKS — answers on a postcard, please, to grandma.

TOETALITARIAN SOCKS

It may have been the sight of the barefoot masses that inspired Karl Marx, but the Revolution has done little for Soviet feet. The Soviet press has reported a chronic socks shortage. The newspaper *Lit Gazeta* investigated sock-lessness. It found it was the fault of the civil servants whose job it is to estimate how many pairs of socks a man needs a year, and to fix the production norms accordingly. The clerks underestimated. They calculated that Soviet Man needed six pairs of socks a year. The real figure should have been eight. Hence the gap.

None the less, those frank admissions on socklessness in Russia were eagerly seized upon by Western observers as a sign that the government-controlled Soviet press might be getting more critical. If they were prepared to expose their bare feet to the eyes of the world, one could only guess the im-plications for The Arms Race. In fact, the great Soviet socks shortage is a long-running scandal. Which is why Soviet di-plomats return home from London with dozens and dozens of chain-store socks.

---

footnote Russian conscripts do not wear socks at all.

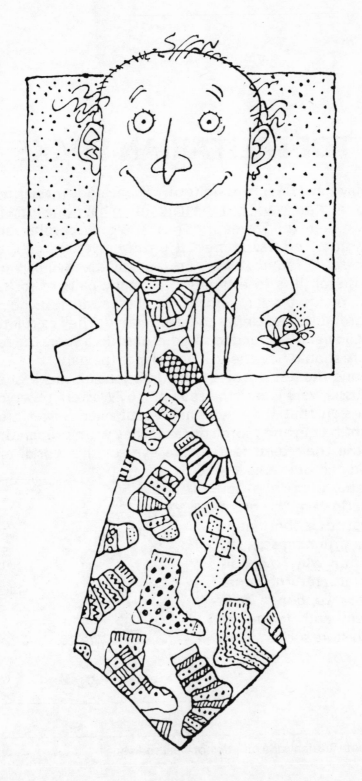

INSTANT SOCK TREATMENT

Such is the overwhelming strength of the socks urge in men that they demand a clean pair each morning – even at weekends. This is not always possible or convenient.

Every now and again (at least twice a week, actually) a chap faces a major emergency. He is desperate for socks, but cannot find a thing to put on. To avert an angry scene or a frantic rummage which will result in a fall-out roughly equivalent to a small nuclear explosion, try some INSTANT SOCK TREATMENT. In a crisis, take whatever footwear is immediately to hand, ie the same pair of socks that he was wearing yesterday, or the day before, and apply one of these tried and tested remedies:

Lay the socks on an ironing board, and spray the outsides with spray-on starch. Then iron. If you are lucky, this will give the socks the superficial appearance of having been properly laundered.

Very smelly socks present a slightly different problem. Pale-coloured socks respond quite well to talcum powder. Turn the sock inside out on your hand and rub some powder well in, and shake vigorously to remove surplus. Then turn it right side out, and iron.

Damp socks dry much more quickly if you use a hair dryer, putting them on your hand rather than the central heating radiator.

SOCKS TIPS FOR SLOBS

Best candidate for the short sharp sock treatment is the pair at the bottom of the laundry basket – the ones he was wearing *last* week. Empirical research indicates that the characteristics of the used sock – smell, sweat, lack of elasticity – decline rather than increase over time. With any luck you might get away with not having to wash any socks at all.

SOCKS ETIQUETTE

You cannot just have socks ANYWHERE. There are some occasions when you should have no socks at all, because it simply isn't the done thing.

WHEN IN BED. Wearing socks in bed is most ungentlemanly, particularly in company since it creates an atmosphere of impermanence not conducive to a satisfactory partnership. A man who wears socks in bed is frequently described as 'a heel'.

WHEN ON THE BEACH. Sand and socks are not a comfortable combination though you can nearly always spot an enthusiastic pair struggling underfoot.

WHEN IN THE SHOWER. You run the risk of shrinkage.

WHEN IN A MONASTERY. SOCKular activities are frowned on. Monks are not supposed to have socks, are they?

WHEN NOT WEARING ANYTHING ELSE IN THE COMPANY OF THE OPPOSITE SEX – unless you want to make yourself a laughing sock, of course.

ELECTRIC SOCKS

Attempts have been made over the years to find a satisfactory solution to the problem of cold feet by developing electric socks. Early efforts included a pair made in New York with warming coils of wire woven into the material and powered by batteries. These proved cumbersome and uncomfortable because the batteries had to be worn on a belt and the lead wires ran down the leg to the socks. Modern versions are also powered by batteries attached to the socks themselves. The main disadvantage is that the batteries have a short life and constantly need replacing.

SOCKS AND POLITICS

Politicians have to be very careful about their socks life —
if they choose to be flamboyant in matters of socks, they
should keep them under wraps in case of scandal. For
instance, when Dr Rainer Barzel was a candidate for the
German Chancellorship, a firm of public relations advisers suggested that a change of socks would increase his
popularity at the polls. Dr Barzel's habit of wearing
white socks all the time was considered to be det-
rimental to his image. He refused to change into any of
the hundred pairs of black socks his advisers sent him. Dr
Barzel has never been heard of since.

STRIKING SOCKS

Are clean socks a Right Of Man? Trade union officials were called in to negotiate with Manchester Corporation after a dozen council electricians went on strike in a dispute over socks. One of their members had been fired after complaints from a tenant that he had washed two pairs of socks in her bathroom when he came to do repairs. The elderly tenant said, 'I thought I could smell something strange. Then out came this man with his socks.'

footnote SMELLYSOCKS BRIGADE – General description of anyone on The Left (Labour politicians, Trade Union leaders, etc). This happy phrase was allegedly coined by Mr Denis Thatcher in his _Dear Bill_ letters in _Private Eye_.

PRE-MARITAL SOCKS
A BACHELOR'S GUIDE

Can you have socks before marriage?
    Yes – but pick a mate with an accommodating washing machine.

How often should you have socks?
    At least once a day – but twice is not abnormal.

Does size matter?
    Most socks will stretch to fit.

Can socks turn you blind?
    Only if you put them over your head.

Should you share socks?
    Comparisons are sometimes odorous.

Is casual socks a good idea?
    Only at weekends on the golf course.

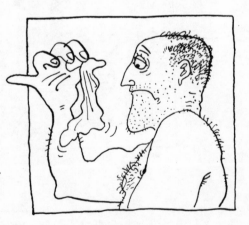

Should you take precautions?
    Unless you want the patter of tiny feet.

Can you prolong socks?
    By hand washing all over very gently.

Smelly socks can give an unfair advantage

DARNING
THE FORGOTTEN ART

Behind every Great Man of Humble Origins there always seems to have been a Wonderful Mother — darning. Indeed, if you fed the memoirs of the Great and Good into a computer to discover the common ingredient for success, you would undoubtedly find that a darning-orientated mother comes pretty near the top of the list. What is it about the memory of mothers darning socks that makes men sentimental? Darning has gone out of fashion owing to the popularity of artificial fibres and the economics of mass production. Now you can afford to throw socks away as soon as they wear thin. Men, of course, consider the demise of darning to be a feminist statement. But perhaps this, like so many other manifestations of progress, has left a gaping emotional hole in our lives that needs to be filled.

To darn you need:

    Matching wool
    A mushroom (not the edible variety)
    A darning needle
    Elastoplast
    An extra finger or two.
    An IQ of around 2

Darning is *not* the same as just stitching something up, despite what many people nowadays believe. If you just sew over a hole in a pair of socks, your partner will end up with cramped toes and blisters. The sock will be too small. Darning is more like weaving. You create a darn by running the wool up and down, and then sideways, over and under to fill the hole. *The loop* is crucial in darning. You leave a small bit of extra wool loose at the edges when you darn, so that when the sock is put on again there is plenty of give at the sides. Do you wonder why nobody does it now?

EXTRA-MARITAL SOCKS

Every now and again a man is tempted by the possibilities of EXTRA MARITAL SOCKS. The signs are easy to spot:

He has a spring in his step.

Strange new socks appear in the laundry basket.

He comes home with one or both socks missing.

He does not come home at all.

There are a number of reasons why a man may feel the need for extra marital socks:

He does not get enough socks at home.

InSOCKurity – if he was deprived of love, affection and a fresh pair of socks every morning as a child he may in adult life feel the need to grab at any socks on offer.

Boredom – he may get fed up with the same old kind of socks. Buy him a pair in bright canary yellow or purple, guaranteed to revive a flagging socks life.

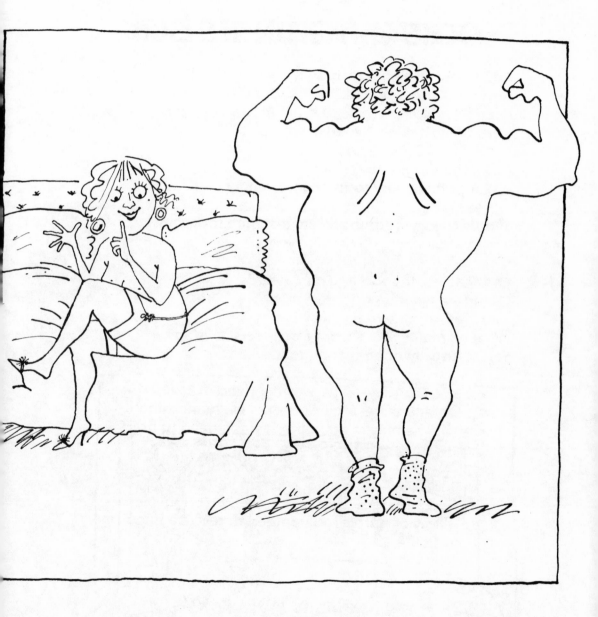

SOCKS & THE SINGLE GIRL

Advice from Helen Girly Brawn.

Is it OK for women to be as keen on socks as men?
Absolutely. It takes two to make a pair.

How long should socks last?
A really satisfactory couple can go on forever.

Should I always respond to his demand for socks?
Yes – with a smile.

Can I have both socks and my career?
Get an au pair.

What do men REALLY want from a relationship?
Socks – usually.

FLARED SOCKS

A group of Edinburgh men were saved by their socks after being adrift in the North Sea on a dinghy for eight hours. The Aberdeen lifeboat spotted them after one of the men signalled by removing his socks, soaking them in petrol, tying them to an oar and setting them alight.

ARRESTING SOCKS

Scotland Yard's museum contains a pair of dark blue socks unique in British legal history. They have foot-prints INSIDE. They helped convict a burglar so anxious to avoid leaving fingerprints or footprints that he wore gloves and put socks OVER his shoes. He made one fatal error. After raiding the house, he took the socks off and left them in the garden. The police found them, and discovered that inside there was a perfect set of footprints formed when mud seeped through the wool to the rigid soles of his shoes. The burglar was later arrested when he tried to rob another house – and was found to be wearing shoes that matched the footprints in the socks he left at his earlier theft.

AWAYDAY SOCKS

British Rail had a one-day socks promotion at Euston station, London. Footsore commuters were invited to leave their socks to be washed free of charge and picked up that evening on their way home. Anyone who could not face a day in the office with bare feet was invited to borrow a pair from British Rail.

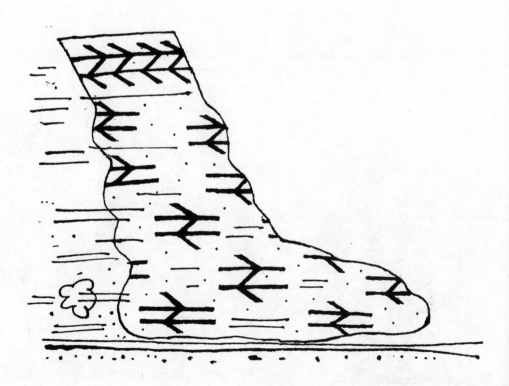

SOCK EXCHANGE

The landlord of The Three Tuns public house near Nottingham opened Britain's first SOCK EXCHANGE. One or two evenings a month, regulars are invited to bring their odd socks with them when they come for a pint. They swap socks to make up a matching pair. The socks on offer are displayed on a big listings board, and the landlord wears a pin-stripe suit and bowler hat for the occasion.

ROYAL SOCK UP

The Duke of Edinburgh appears to have put his foot in it
again by suggesting that Britain's businessmen should
'pull their socks up' in world markets. Leading indus-
trialists were puzzled by the precise meaning of the
Duke's outburst which comes at a time when exports are
at an all-time high and business is booming. 'I don't
think our socks are in any way inferior to the Japs' or
Germans',' said one leading industrialist. 'In fact, I
would go so far as to say that our socks hold up well
against the competition.' Another told me, 'I don't see
what socks have to do with it. Our chaps can think very
fast on their feet.'

The Duke's remarks have apparently offended The
Federation of Sock Manufacturers. A spokesperson told
me, 'The Royal Family should give us support, not drag
us down. Our chaps need encouragement – most of them
are stretched to the limit.'

A Palace aide later suggested that the Duke's remarks, made at a World Life Fund Open Evening, had
been taken out of context. He said 'Someone is shooting
a line. This is all most unpheasant.'

HIGH SOCKCIETY

SOCKS PROBE HORROR

THE IDENTITY of the so-far unnamed 'sockless man', a picture of whose bare feet became crucial evidence in one of the most lurid divorce battles of the century, is about to be disclosed, I can reveal.

A JUST-COMPLETED study, *Socks Lives of the Rich and Famous*, apparently includes dramatic new evidence as to the size, shape and colour of the feet that have puzzled gossip columnists for decades. Until now the only clue to the man's identity was the sock he left behind him in haste – long, black silk, size 10, actually – which created a furore when presented in court as exhibit A. The other one of the pair was never found, despite reported sightings from places as diverse as Brazil and South Africa.

FOR YEARS after the sock went missing, it was assumed it had done the decent thing and committed socksicide – but the author claims it was dug up by accident in the garden of a house just a few doors from the scene of the incident that socked Britain all those years ago. Now the sock, and the identity of the famous foot, face exposure. I can reveal ALL – in tomorrow's column.

SOCKS PARLOURS

THE ESTABLISHMENT is quaking in its boots following revelations in certain Sunday newspapers of regular visits to socks parlours by well-known feet from the world of show business, politics and even – it is hinted – the *Royal Circle*. I can reveal that the socks parlour in question – within easy walking distance of the Palace – advertises itself as a perfectly respectable chiropodist's practice. But behind the scenes there are bosomy blonde assistants, highly trained in the art of socks massage, and prepared to take their wealthy clients' feet in hand for fees of anything up to £100 an hour. As one 'footmaiden' told me, 'It's all perfectly respectable and above board. I don't see anything wrong about men paying for socks.'

TODAY IN THE SOCKMARKET

There was a scent of panic in the air on the London Sock Exchange yesterday. Dealers voted with their feet and prices took to their heels. At the end of the day, socks were well down and still falling.

Footsie closed 30 points off at 1,200, and traders were at full stretch trying to keep pace with selling orders. Shock news that President Sockarno might walk away from vital oil talks left the market sweating. Any rise in prices could leave the oil majors desperately short of socks, though the balance sheet benefits of sock appreciation could leave them looking smart. The impact on their profit and loss accounts will depend on whether they use LOFO – the last on, first off method of accounting. Anything else would tear a nasty hole in earnings.

Lord Feet of Stephens has announced a bid for Toeser Kemsley. He wants to merge it with Tottenham Sock-spur, the football club. Lord Feet says; 'The Achilles heel of British socker is our inability to stand on our own two feet. I want to kick some life into it.' The merged group will be called Toeser Sockspur.

Amalgamated Boots have been appointed sole agents for the new Australian talc deposit at Wooliwearra. Chairman Sir Nicholas Tickleus said, 'This will shake 'em. I'm delighted. We'll be stocking up.'

There was an attempt at contango business in a thin market in international loan socks, but officials put their foot down, fearing a nasty run. Tea-time rumours of a dawn raid brought calls for sock suspension pending clarification. Unless there is a new issue in the morning, socks will open higher.

RHYMING SOCKS

Hall & Son, one of the UK's oldest sock-makers, deal with customer complaints in rhyme:

From Mrs Gaylor, Milton Keynes

'The socks enclosed are tattered and torn
And four times only have they been worn
My husband's hose is my despair
As darning holes I cannot bear.
So please replace under guarantee
And let the new pair be satisfactory.'

From Hall & Son

'Oh Mrs Gaylor,
What a failure,
And in Milton Keynes of all places.
No, please don't repair –
Accept this new pair
And excuse the blush on our faces.
We're perfectly sure
This pair will endure
And show up the one it replaces;
So thus in MK
Mr G will then say,
Our guarantee went
        through its paces.'

SOCKS SUMMONS

A stallholder in London's Petticoat Lane was summonsed for selling men's socks when his licence said he could sell only stockings. The case turned on the definition of a sock. The case against him collapsed when he produced a dictionary which defined a sock as 'a short stocking not reaching the knee.'

SOCKS AID

A Manchester children's charity couldn't understand why people kept sending them socks from around the world. During one week the postman delivered 1,500 pairs – some odd, some with holes, some new. Then it was discovered that the secretary who typed the charity's appeal letter on behalf of a local hospital had put 'sock' instead of 'rock' for the children to eat. Socks are not nearly so tasty.

footnote A pair of sailing socks worn by former Tory Prime Minister, Mr Edward Heath, raised £3 at a charity auction. Organizers said that the demand for Mr Heath's socks was 'disappointing'.

SOCKS
OPERA

He may be so romantic
At the opera in a box,
But he ain't so darned attractive
When you're washing out his socks.

SOCKS LETTERS

Ask a silly question and you get an even sillier answer —
even from readers of *The Financial Times*. One asked
why socks ended up single rather than in pairs. Here are
some of the replies:

'Wives may destroy a sock in order to pave the way for
another cheap unoriginal birthday or Christmas present.
But I wonder if the International Wool Secretariat may
not have a secret division (SOX perhaps) to see that
every other sock is soaked in a special chemical so that
on the third or fourth washing it dissolves — thus subtly
promoting increased sales and rising wool consumption.
Significantly, wool prices are on a rising trend.'

'The phenomenon of the errant sock is by no means
new. Years ago in my university hall of residence, a
twin-tub washing machine defied the attempts of the
service engineer to render it operative. Successive waves
of students — mechanical, electrical and civil engineers,
even dental students — examined it. Eventually a law stu-
dent realized that its drain was blocked — by a single sock.'

'An interesting theory a few years ago suggested that socks are the larval stage during a life cycle. One sock is destined to remain at the larval stage. Its sibling grows up to become a coat hanger. If Mr Moss keeps count of the hangers in his wardrobe he will find, as I do, that their increase is in direct proportion to the disappearance of his socks.'

'Mr Moss's experience is, I am afraid, typical of many small investors who have been drawn into the laundromat following "Big Splash", hoping to clean up in an afternoon. Reading the small print makes it clear that a single sock is the standard commission rate on all "loads", to use the correct term. Mr Moss should consider himself lucky. There are many recent examples of whole shirts being lost.'

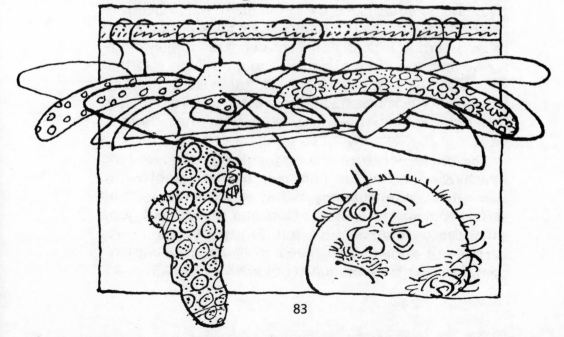

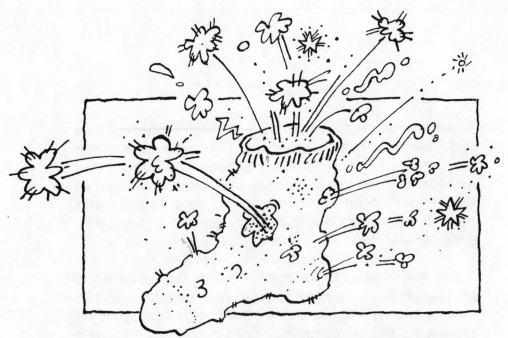

'Nearly thirty years ago, as an articled clerk I was sent on an audit to the Slough Trading Estate. (In those days to do an audit there was considered character forming.) The client made many of the solutions which went into washing powders made by all the major manufacturers. In the course of the company's stock-take, I came across a cupboard – locked and considered extremely high-value material. On making my enquiries I was told that this was for a special export solution sent to some western states of the US and to the Argentinian Pampas. Modern cowboys, it seemed, did not like their chaps so stiff that they were wont to stand up on their own. This made them inconvenient for putting into washing machines. The solution had been devised to soften up the chaps. Unfortunately it had a more devastating effect. But so much time, effort and money had gone into the development of this substance that it was decided it should be filtered into ordinary washing powders over the next quarter of a century. . . .'

'On the subject of single socks, this is obviously an important political matter and one which comes up many times at council meetings. It would appear that more socks are devoured by washing machines in Knowsley than elsewhere in the country. The Labour Party blame the Government, saying it is a plot to suppress the workers whilst at the same time giving a boost to the Lancashire textile industry. We in the Conservative Party know better. The socks which are lost by Liberal Party members end up on the feet of SDP members. The likelihood of the original owners ever recreating a matched pair is minuscule.'

'I too have had the same problem as Mr Moss with single socks that have lost their mates. What is needed, if they are to be reunited, is a Sock Exchange run by sockbrokers. There could be a leasing offshoot with convertible loan socks. . . .'

CHRISTMAS SOCKS

However awful or boring they are, *look inside* before chucking them away. Mr Alf Tufnell did not like the socks he got from his mother-in-law as a Christmas present, and exchanged them in a department store for another pair. Only when his mother-in-law asked how he liked the 'little surprise' she had put in the socks did he realize that he had missed the two gold half sovereigns she had tucked away in the toes.

LONG-RUNNING SOCKS

British socks are renowned for their longevity, versatility, and endurance – just so long as they don't get lost in the wash. Perhaps the best example of socks survival was the 40 year-old pair, of UK manufacture, sent to a newspaper. Bought in a Budapest department store in the late 1920s, they emigrated to the US with their owner after surviving the Second World War. Alas, in the mid-1960s the socks, still in full walking order, were inadvertently swallowed by their owner's pet baby boa constrictor. For six weeks the socks were missing, presumed dead, in its entrails until it coughed them up and they were retrieved by their grateful wearer. Amazingly the socks had survived their dramatic encounter with the snake's gastric juices, intact, but slightly stained.

CLASSIFIED SOCKS

£1 per foot for personal advertisers

£1.25 per foot for business advertisers

SOCKS AID

No more panting and wheezing. The FOOT BUTLER provides socks support for the mature wearer who has difficulty getting his socks on in the morning. Two long-handled padded clamps – made of 100 percent reinforced galvanized steel – £5 a pair. (Post and packing extra.) Cheque or Postal Order to PO Box 100, SOCKIHALL STREET, GLASGOW.

TOETAL BLISS this winter with HOT SOCKS – small removable electrically powered batteries. No plugs no wires – all colours available. Send stamped addressed socks to WATT SOCKS LTD, PO BOX 15.

Cure SWEATY FEET nature's way. Wear rubber socks from ACHILLES HEAL, Whimsy Street, London N13. Matching nightwear also available.

PAIRSONAL SERVICES

Give your FEET a TREAT – make an appointment with our team of qualified foot masseurs. Toe kissing a speciality. THE SOCKS PARLOUR, phone 01 666 3333 and ask for SONIA. Credit cards accepted.

Looking for something a little EX-SOCKTIC? Tall black slender ribbed silk dying to be handwashed nightly. PO BOX 606.

ENRICH YOUR SOCKS LIFE

SOCKS SWAP INTERNATIONAL A new organization designed for the discerning sockphisticate wants to help you make the perfect match. Phone 00090 86 for details.

Hang out your fantasies on SOCKS-LINE – live private conversation fantasy of your choice, 0863 972.

SOCKSAGRAMS —— say it with feet. Also WPC's, Tarzans, Nuns, Schoolgirls, Rambos, Gorillas available. Tel. 0802 653.

Wax socks candle – light up his life with the perfect Christmas gift. £2.95 payable to Willywax Enterprises, Fleetwood, Lancs.

Get socks off your chest – experienced socks therapist can sort out your problems, PO BOX 106.

LONELY SOCKS COLUMN

Warm woolly well-used seeks similar mature partnership. Love of darning essential. PO Box 994.

Dashing red-spotted needs sole mate for occasional foot frolics. PO Box 888.

Slightly shrunken badly-treated seeks friendlier foot. Sincere replies only please, PO Box 222.

Barefoot male, (35, public school) seeks 25 year-old graduate with working washing machine view concerts, opera, theatre, socks etc., PO Box 351.

ARGYLE SOCKS

The awful, multi-coloured, diamond-patterned Argyle socks, beloved by golfers, have even penetrated the tiny isolated kingdom of Bhutan, where they are part of the hillmen's traditional costume. Quite how the Argyle got its name, let alone clambered several thousand feet up the Himalayas is a bit of a mystery.

Scottish Highlanders wore tartan socks in the mid-19th century. This then became fashionable with those who went to Scotland to shoot grouse. The style was not invented by the rather grand Argyll family (different spelling) although, in the 1950s, the then duke was paid to endorse the socks. The subsequent confusion over the origins of the Argyle still irritates the duchess (of Argyll), who told a journalist despairingly, 'One doesn't want, you know, to be known for a sock.' Quite so.

SHARK SOCK SHOCK

Shark fishermen stuff old socks with rotting fish guts and trail them behind their boats. Sharks have a highly developed sense of smell and quickly pick up the scent. They follow the trail until they find the baited hooks of the fishermen.

THE SOCKS WAR

'Sex and socks are not compatible'
Angela Carter

But then again, can a man really expect BOTH?

Next to house prices, socks are the one feeture virtually guaranteed to stimulate lively, informed discussion at dinner parties. More important, socks are one of the few topics on which men and women will almost certainly be divided, and over which they can have a decent argument. From a male point of view, socks seem to have a symbolic significance which stretches way beyond just keeping a chap's feet warm. The reason is very simple. In the age of equality, Marks & Sparks ready-prepared meals, working mothers, multiple orgasms, what else do they have that is uniquely theirs?

THE BIOLOGICAL IMPERATIVE Modern man's socks behaviour is directly related to his primitive animal past.

MAN THE HUNTER In primitive societies, the male of the species had a highly developed hunting instinct. He needed it for survival in an inhospitable environment where men would go out in the morning and search for the day's food. Now that women hunt each day through Sainsbury's, this obsolete masculine urge finds expression in the daily ritual of tracking down the socks – or usually, *the other sock*.

MAN THE PEACOCK In the animal kingdom, it is usually the male of the species with the brighter plumage and colouring, though sartorial exhibitionism of this kind is nowadays frowned upon by humans. The female is expected to dress to kill. Men are expected to wear dull suits. The one *accepted* area where men may indulge their repressed desire for individuality is the foot. Hence we find merchant bankers wearing pin-stripes and *red socks*, or politicians wearing *pink socks* – even the (very) odd accountant turning out in *dayglo green*.

THE DOMINANT MALE Men like to have women at their feet. In modern society the man's insistence on socks is a hangover from earlier forms of behaviour (Anglo-Saxon toe kissing, for instance), now ritualized in order to fit contemporary life. Traditionally, socks implies subservience.

LAST THOUGHT

LOVE IS . . .
NEVER HAVING
TO SAY BUY BUY